Steg and the Tar Pit

A play by Alison Hawes
Illustrated by Lalalimola

Characters

Don

Steg

Dac

Ig

Plod

Narrator

Narrator: Steg is at the river bank with his friends.

Steg: What shall we do today?

Plod: Let's all splash in the river!

Ig: We did that last week.

Don: I'm sick of splashing!

Dac: Me too!

Ig: Let's make a den in the forest.

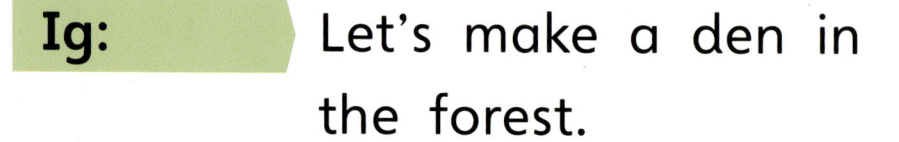

Don: No, we did that last week, too.

Steg: Let's go to the tar pit then!

Plod: We can't go there!

Ig: Plod is right. We can't play in the tar pit.

Dac: We might fall into the tar.

Don: Yes, and then we might get stuck!

Narrator: But Steg runs off to the tar pit.

Plod: Come back, Steg! Come back!

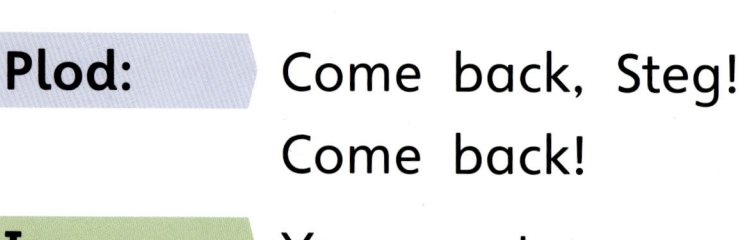

Ig: You are too near the pit!

Don: You might fall into the tar!

Steg: Look at me! Look at me!

Dac: Look out, Steg!

Narrator: Just then, Steg falls into the tar pit.

Steg: Help! Help! I am stuck in the tar!

Don: Keep still, Steg. We'll get you out.

Plod: But how? How can we help him?

Ig: We can make a raft. It will float on the tar.

Narrator: So they make a raft from wood.

Dac: We'll push the raft into the tar pit now, Steg.

Don: Get on it when it comes to you.

Steg: I can't! I'm stuck!

Plod: Yes you can. Just keep cool.

Dac: It's coming. That's it, Steg!

Ig: You can do it!

Steg: Yes! I **can** get on the raft!

Narrator: Steg's friends pull him back to dry land.

Dac: Get that tar off you, Steg!

Don: Yes, you smell!

Steg: Thank you for getting me out!

Narrator: Steg hugs his friends.

Dac: Yuck! Now we need to get the tar off us, too!

Ig: But how can we get it off?

15

Don: Let's all splash in the river.

Plod: Yes! Just like I said in the first place. Let's all splash in the river!